STORMS AND PEOPLE

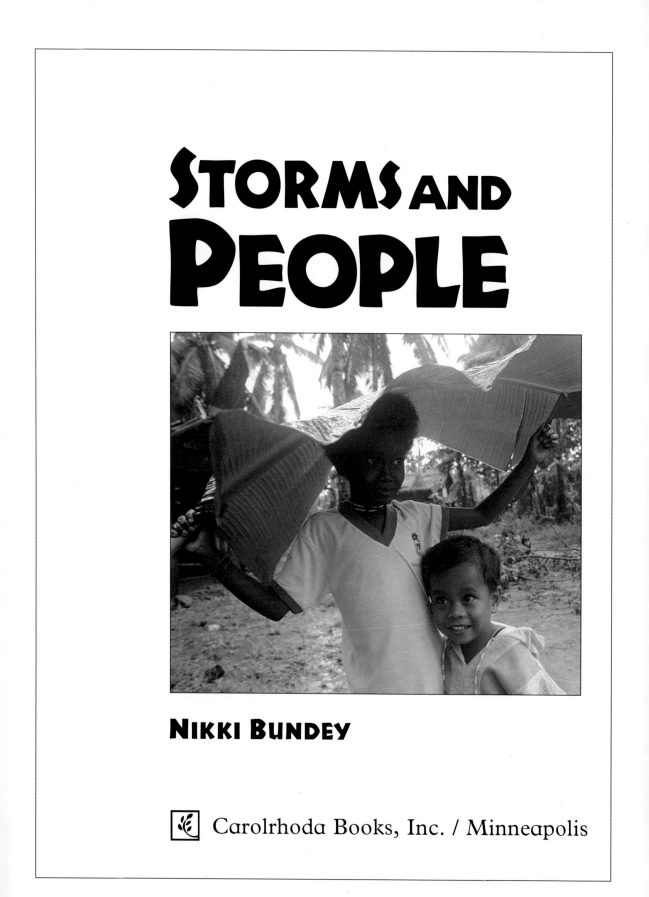

NIKKI BUNDEY

Carolrhoda Books, Inc. / Minneapolis

First American edition published in 2001 by
Carolrhoda Books, Inc.

All the words that appear in **bold** type are explained
in the glossary that starts on page 30.

Wilkinson—cover (inset) left / Pern 27 / Hutchison Picture Library; Jonathan Pile 10 /
Yann Arthus-Bertrand 12, 15t, 25b / John Walmsley 23t / Simon Shepheard 25t /
Stephen Hird 26t / Impact Photos; 13t / Peter Newark's Western Americana; Martin
Wendler 13b / G.I. Bernard 16b / TSADO/NCDC/NOAA 29b / NHPA; Shezad
Noorani—cover (inset) right, 18 / Mark Edwards—title page, 19b / Kent Wood 4 /
Martha Cooper 7 / Boris Rostami-Rabet 19t, 23b / Gerard and Margi Moss 21t / Jean-
Luc and F Ziegler 26b / NOAA 29t / Still Pictures; Streano/Havens—cover
(background) / J Greenberg 5t / J Sweeney 5b / NASA 6t / P Treanor 6b / Viesti
Collection 8 / M Jelliffe 9t / H Rogers 9b, 15b / M Lee 11 / Archive Photos 14 /
Australian Picture Library 16t / N and J Wiseman 17 / Picturesque 20 / J Ringland 21b
/ D Saunders 22 / Mike Smith 24 / J Stanley 28 / TRIP.

Illustrations by Artistic License/Tracy Fennell, Janie Pirie

Carolrhoda Books, Inc.
A division of Lerner Publishing Group
241 First Avenue North
Minneapolis, MN 55401 U.S.A.

Website address: www.lernerbooks.com

A ZOË BOOK

Copyright © 2001 Zoë Books Limited. Originally produced in 2001 by Zoë Books
Limited, Winchester, England

Library of Congress Cataloging-in-Publication Data

Bundey, Nikki, 1948–
    Storms and people / by Nikki Bundey
        p. cm.—(The science of weather)
        Includes index.
        ISBN 1-57505-499-X (lib. bdg. : alk. paper)
    1. Storms—Juvenile literature. 2. Weather—Juvenile literature.
    [1. Storms.] I. Title. II. Series: Bundey, Nikki, 1948– The science
    of weather.
    QC941.3.B855   2001
    551.55—dc21   00-010088

Printed in Italy by Grafedit SpA
Bound in the United States of America
1 2 3 4 5 6—OS—06 05 04 03 02 01

CONTENTS

STORM WARNING

Dark clouds pile up in the sky. The wind rises and soon begins to howl around the buildings. Rain drives down, splashing against window panes. Suddenly, a great flash of **lightning** forks across the sky. Then a loud clap of **thunder** shakes the house.

It's best not to go outside. Tree branches are crashing into the street, and it could be dangerous!

Lightning forks over the city of Tucson, Arizona. The power of the weather affects our everyday lives in many ways.

Water floods the roads after a violent rainstorm. Storms can destroy houses, prevent travel, and even threaten human life.

Storms can bring violent weather conditions. Long ago, people believed that storms were a sign that the gods and goddesses were angry. The ancient Romans believed that a god named Jupiter hurled thunder and lightning at humans as a punishment or a warning. The Vikings believed that the god Thor made thunder with his great hammer.

In modern times, scientists know why storms occur. Weather science is called **meteorology**.

Many Native American peoples believed in a powerful spirit called the thunderbird. Lightning was said to shoot from its eyes. Its beating wings made the sound of thunder.

WHY IS IT STORMY?

Air, or **atmosphere**, surrounds the earth's surface like a blanket. The air is made up of **gases**. They press down on the surface of the planet. This force is called **air pressure**.

To understand storms, we must find out what happens when gases heat up and cool down. Gases rise when the sun warms them. Then cooler gases rush in below to take their place. This movement creates winds. Winds pick up moisture from the oceans.

Photographs of the earth from space clearly show the weather systems circling our planet.

This heavy rainstorm is in Manila on the Philippine Islands. Winds called **monsoons** have carried the rain across the Indian Ocean to Southeast Asia.

Winter brings heavy storms of snow, called blizzards, to the islands of Japan. Snow is fun for children, but it can cause many problems. Can you think of some?

Moisture from the oceans sometimes changes, or **evaporates**, into a gas called **water vapor**. Then the water vapor cools and **condenses**. It turns back into **liquid** water or into **solid** ice. Water and ice crystals fall from the sky as rain and snow.

Pressure systems spin and push each other around the earth, sometimes creating storms. Low-pressure systems bring cloudy, gloomy weather. High-pressure systems bring clear, sunny weather.

DISASTER ZONES

Many storms bring high winds, or **gales**. Some of the most powerful winds are called tornadoes, or twisters. They spin around at high speed.

Tropical storms are huge thunderstorms. They form over the sea and batter coasts and islands. In the Atlantic Ocean, the fiercest tropical storms are called hurricanes. These storms are called typhoons in the Pacific Ocean and cyclones in the Indian Ocean.

Lightning's great heat can destroy entire buildings and set forests on fire. Lightning is made of **electricity**, which can kill people.

Rainstorms often cause floods, which can turn hard soil into soft mud. After a cyclone, this river in Madagascar, off the coast of Africa, is full of muddy water.

High winds can drive down torrents of rain, creating floods or blizzards of heavy snow. Winds can whip up huge waves at sea.

Electrical storms start when electric charges build up inside clouds. Then, an electric current—a bolt of lightning—travels between the cloud and the ground. The lightning heats up the air, creating a **shock wave** that we call thunder.

After a typhoon in Taiwan, Asia, the hard soil turned into soft mud. It ran down the hill and swept away part of the road. Workers are repairing the damage.

9

STAYING ALIVE

The human body can survive in extreme weather conditions. Our skin is **waterproof**, and we can swim. We can grip things with our hands, and we can run fast. When danger threatens, our bodies release a natural chemical called **adrenaline**. It helps pump blood straight to our muscles, so that we can move quickly.

Humans are also fragile. Our bones can break. During floods and storms at sea, people might fall in the water and drown.

During storms, people might run for shelter. Adrenaline surges through their bodies to give them the power to run fast.

A walk in the mountains can turn into a disaster if you are not properly prepared. Storms may bring high winds, rain, hail, or snow. You will need food and warm, waterproof clothing.

People also need to stay warm. If a person is lost during a blizzard or washed into the sea during a storm, his or her body **temperature** may drop to the danger level. This condition is called **hypothermia**.

See for Yourself

- Imagine that you are going for a walk in the mountains.
- How might you find out what the weather will be like?
- Make a list of things that you might take to:
  - keep dry
  - stay warm
  - find your way
  - alert rescuers if you're lost
  - help in a medical emergency
  - avoid hunger and thirst

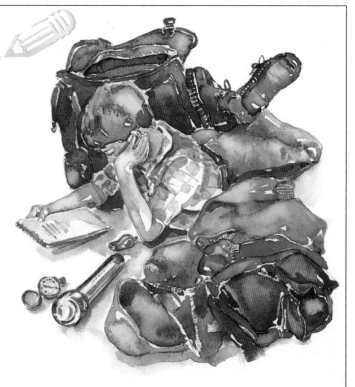

FARMERS FACE RUIN

Farmers need rain for their crops, but a heavy storm may flood the land. Flooding ruins most crops and strands cattle and sheep. Rice is one crop that is well suited to storms, however. It grows naturally in flooded river valleys.

High winds can flatten fields of wheat, making them impossible to harvest. Tornadoes can destroy farm buildings. High winds can also whip up desert sand, carrying dust storms to fertile farmland.

Floods have stranded these cattle in Florida after a hurricane.

In the 1930s, high winds deposited dust over a large area of American farmland. The farmers planted windbreaks to keep the soil from blowing away.

High winds and heavy rains can wear down, or **erode**, farmland. They blow or wash away the rich, fertile topsoil from the land's surface. Only the rock below remains.

Hedges and trees protect farmland from storms. They act as a **windbreak**, shielding the land from gales. Their roots trap moisture and anchor loose soil.

Forests once covered this part of Brazil. When people cut down the forests, there were no trees to keep tropical storms from washing away the soil.

A ROOF OVER YOUR HEAD

People have always needed to take shelter from storms. Caves have given shelter to people since prehistoric times. However, caves often flood during storms. Rainwater seeps down through rocks and fills up underground streams.

Some people use tents for shelter. Tents can be moved easily. To stand up to storms, tents need strong poles to make them firm and **guy ropes** to keep them from blowing away.

A tornado can destroy homes and buildings. Basements provide the best protection during tornadoes.

People build underground shelters to protect themselves against the full force of tornadoes. If people stay above ground, they may be hurt or killed if their houses collapse.

The strip of metal at the top of this building is called a lightning rod. It is made of copper, and it protects the building from lightning. Copper can **conduct**, or carry, electricity. If lightning strikes, the electricity travels through the copper and down a cable into the ground. It does not damage the building.

Skyscrapers must be strong enough to stand up to powerful winds and hurricanes. They are built to sway, or bend very slightly, with the wind. Structures that are flexible, or bendy, are more likely to survive a storm.

In areas where storms are common, people usually build villages and towns in sheltered valleys. The buildings need strong **foundations** and roofs to stand up to the force of the wind.

15

ROADS AT RISK

Traveling is dangerous in stormy weather. High winds can blow down trees, crushing cars or blocking roads.

Tall vehicles such as trucks and buses offer the most **wind resistance**. They might overturn in high winds. Low, **streamlined** vehicles pass through the wind more easily. Large tires have big **treads** that grip the road surface, keeping the tires from slipping.

In Australia, the roads are underwater after a storm. Heavy rainstorms can wash away or collapse roads, especially roads that are not built with hard surfaces.

Falling trees crushed many cars during a recent storm in England.

Strong winds can make it dangerous to cross high bridges. Instruments that measure wind speed are attached to bridges. These instruments are called **anemometers**. When the wind is too strong for safety, the bridge is closed to traffic.

Roads must be properly drained so that the surface does not flood. Some areas get sudden rushes of water, called flash floods. People must build storm sewers to take the water away.

Bridges are put under all sorts of strain and stress during storms. Waves may batter the piers, or upright posts. Gales may shake bridges until upper towers fall down.

See for Yourself

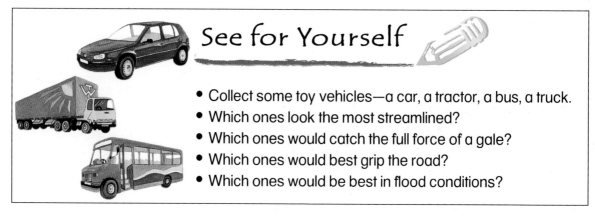

- Collect some toy vehicles—a car, a tractor, a bus, a truck.
- Which ones look the most streamlined?
- Which ones would catch the full force of a gale?
- Which ones would best grip the road?
- Which ones would be best in flood conditions?

FLOOD ALERT!

Rainstorms and monsoons may make rivers burst their banks and spill over the countryside. Rough seas and high **tides** can flood low-lying coasts. Tides are caused by the force of **gravity** pulling on the earth from the moon and the sun.

Water may wash away soil and make the foundations of buildings collapse. If drains and sewers flood, there is a risk to people's health. **Germs** in the dirty water might cause diseases.

Boats can help rescue people from their homes during a flood. **Sandbags** are used to make walls to hold back floodwater. **Pumps** can help drain away the floodwater.

This river burst its banks during a hurricane and damaged this village in Nicaragua. In many parts of the world, people build homes on long poles called stilts. This way, the homes stay above the level of the floodwater.

Low-lying areas need protection against floods, such as barriers to hold back the water. These have to be very strong to hold back **water pressure**, waves, or fast-running tides.

Barriers can be seawalls or great banks called **dikes**. High banks are built along rivers that flood often, such as the Mississippi River. These banks are called **levees**.

The Thames River flows through London, England. When storms blow in from the North Sea, the river could burst its banks and flood the city. During a flood warning, ten big steel gates, such as the one here, rise from the riverbed to seal off the waterway.

STORMS AT SEA

Storms at sea can be terrifying. Gales pile up high waves. Powerful ocean **currents** and tides drive the waves along.

Some gigantic waves are called **tsunamis**. They are caused by **earthquakes** under the sea. They travel very fast and can flood coasts and harbors.

During storms, ships could be wrecked on rocky coasts. Lighthouses use powerful lights and sometimes sounds to warn ships of danger.

A typhoon has driven these ships onto rocks on the coast of Korea. The ships are damaged and cannot float. Waves will damage them even more.

During gales, ships anchor behind islands or headlands for shelter. The land acts as a windbreak. In the South China Sea, ships try to reach special storm harbors. These have been built to protect ships from typhoons.

During a storm, boats pitch and toss with the movement of the waves. This motion may make us seasick. Why? It upsets our system of balance, which is controlled by fluid inside our ears.

Boats and people can float in the sea because the water pushes up against them, holding them up. Rafts and **life jackets** make it easier for people to stay afloat in a stormy sea.

FLYING INTO DANGER

Storms can be a big problem for air traffic. Hurricanes can destroy airplanes on the ground. Blizzards and dust storms can keep planes from taking off. The sea often floods low-lying airports, like the one on the Maldive Islands in the Indian Ocean.

Airplanes use air currents when they take off and fly. If a strong **tailwind** follows the plane, the aircraft will need less fuel. With a strong **head wind**, the plane will use more fuel.

A hurricane has hit this airport in Jamaica. It has lifted an airplane into the trees between the runway and the road.

All pilots must check weather conditions before they take off. Blizzards or dust storms could prevent a safe landing.

High above the clouds, an airplane avoids the worst of the weather conditions at the earth's surface. The main problem high in the air is **turbulence**. The plane may bounce and bump as the wind speed and air pressure change rapidly. Fasten your safety belts!

When **volcanoes** like this one erupt, they are a real danger to aircraft. They often create massive electrical storms. Volcanoes also throw up clouds of ash. This can choke a jet engine and make a plane crash.

STORM RESCUE

People have to act quickly to save lives during a storm. Supplies and food may be flown in. Roads and railroad tracks need to be cleared. Seawalls need to be repaired. Floodwater needs to be pumped away.

Emergency vehicles include ambulances, lifeboats, and helicopters. Fire engines can pump away water as well as fight fires.

Helicopters have powerful rotors, or blades. The rotors whirl to make the aircraft move up and down or hover over one place. These movements are very important in a storm rescue.

The sailors who rescue people from the sea are very skilled. They practice working as a team to make sure they can rescue people quickly. Lifeboats must have powerful engines to move through rough seas. The boats need to be small to move quickly.

Rescue teams face the same dangers as the people they are rescuing. They need the right equipment to protect themselves. This gear might include life vests and waterproof jackets and boots. Helmets protect the rescuers' heads.

Rescue teams may use tough ropes and powerful **winches** to move heavy objects. They may need powerful lights, **generators** for electricity, and radios to keep in touch with base.

These people are waiting to be rescued during a flood. They will be thirsty and hungry. The rescue team will have to carry them to safety.

POISON STORMS

Storms are natural events, but human-made disasters are not. An oil tanker might run aground and break up during a storm at sea, causing terrible **pollution**.

Sticky, black oil covers the coast and kills wildlife and plants. People try to keep oil from spreading by placing a boom, or floating barrier, around it. They also use **detergents** to help clean up the oil.

Floods raged through this area of Mozambique, Africa. Flooding might become more common if air pollution changes the earth's climate.

In January 2000, an oil tanker named the *Erika* broke up off the coast of Brittany, France. The thick oil and other poisonous chemicals covered the seashore. Thousands of birds were killed.

While some parts of the world have storms, with high winds and heavy rains, other places have **droughts**. They are turning into deserts. In Africa and Asia, dust storms are becoming more common.

Pollution of the air can also hurt the earth. Gases from car exhaust and factories may be causing **global warming**. As temperatures rise, the world is becoming a stormier place.

Many parts of the world have more rain than they used to. Global warming could make the sea levels rise and cause flooding along low-lying coasts.

See for Yourself

- Fill a dishpan with water.
- Pour in some cooking oil.
- Stir the water to make a pretend storm. Do the blobs of oil disappear?
- Try to surround the oil with a large rubber band. This is your "boom."
- Add a drop of dishwashing liquid to the oil. What happens?

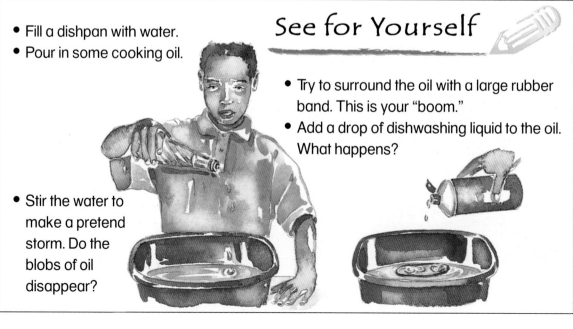

STORM REPORT

Sitting comfortably at home, you can hear **weather forecasts** on TV. Forecasters might warn of tornadoes, hurricanes, and severe storms at sea. Forecasts are made on the Internet, too.

Forecasting storms is an important job. Scientists called meteorologists study the weather. Their forecasts can save lives and protect property. People who need storm warnings include pilots, sailors, farmers, truckers, and hikers. Forecasts help the emergency services plan for disasters.

Big waves in the North Sea could batter this **oil rig**. The engineers who design oil rigs need weather information. The workers who operate the rigs, the supply ship captains who take goods to them, and the helicopter pilots who carry people to the rigs need weather forecasts, too.

Satellites in space track the movements of severe storms such as hurricanes. Images of the storms are sent back to earth. Then meteorologists can predict where the storms will pass next.

Meteorologists mark areas of high and low air pressure on maps. Low-pressure systems often bring stormy weather.

Weather stations on land and ships at sea gather details of weather conditions around the world. Aircraft and spacecraft also send weather information back to earth.

Meteorologists use computers to collect information on storms as they happen and to predict what will happen next. Forecasters warn people when a hurricane, like this one in Florida, is approaching, so that people can move to safety.

GLOSSARY

adrenaline	A natural chemical that helps the body react quickly to stress and danger
air pressure	The force with which air presses down on the earth's surface
anemometer	An instrument used to measure wind speed
atmosphere	The layer of gases around a planet
condense	To turn from a gas into a liquid
conduct	To carry or pass on heat or electricity
current	A movement or flow of air or water
detergent	A soaplike chemical that breaks down oils and fats
dike	A barrier or ditch built to keep back or hold floodwater
drought	A long, dry period with little or no rainfall
earthquake	A shock caused by movements in the earth's crust
electricity	A kind of energy found in nature—in the form of lighting, for instance—and generated as a source of power
erode	To wear away soil or rock
evaporate	To turn from liquid to gas
foundation	An underground structure that anchors a building in the ground
gale	A strong wind; wind moving at 32 to 63 miles per hour
gas	An airy substance that fills any space in which it is contained
generator	A machine used to produce electricity
germ	A living thing that causes disease
global warming	A warming of the earth, possibly caused by air pollution
gravity	The force that pulls objects to the earth
guy rope	A rope or cable used to anchor an object against the wind
head wind	A wind that blows against the front of an aircraft, slowing or lifting it
hypothermia	A condition that occurs when the body's temperature drops to a dangerously low level
levee	A raised bank built to hold water and prevent flooding
life jacket	A vest that helps people float in water

lightning	An electrical current that travels between clouds or between clouds and the ground
liquid	A fluid substance, such as water
meteorology	The scientific study of weather
monsoon	A seasonal rain-bearing wind in southern Asia
oil rig	A huge platform at sea, used in drilling for oil under the ocean
pollution	The poisoning of land, air, or water
pressure system	A huge mass of swirling air. Air rises in low-pressure systems and sinks in high-pressure systems
pump	A machine that helps move or drain away liquids such as water
sandbag	A sack of sand used as a wall or barrier during a flood
satellite	A spacecraft sent up to circle a planet
shock wave	A wave of energy, created by explosion or intense heat
solid	Hard or firm, having a specific shape
streamlined	Slipping easily through the air
tailwind	A wind that blows from behind an aircraft, pushing it forward
temperature	Warmth or coldness, measured in degrees
thunder	A booming or crashing sound created when lightning heats up air
tide	A daily rising and falling of sea levels, caused by the pull of gravity from the moon and the sun
tread	A ridge on a tire that helps it grip the road
tropical	Related to the tropics, the warm regions north and south of the equator
tsunami	A huge wave caused by earthquakes under the sea
turbulence	An unstable condition in the air that causes airplanes to bump and bounce
volcano	An opening in the earth's crust. Gas, ash, and lava blow out of volcanoes from time to time
water pressure	The force with which water presses against an object
waterproof	Able to repel, or keep out, water
water vapor	The gas created when water evaporates
weather forecast	An estimate or prediction of future weather conditions
winch	A reel, powered by hand or by motor, used to haul in lines
windbreak	Something that gives shelter by breaking the force of the wind
wind resistance	The force with which objects withstand the wind

INDEX